The Gift of Gabby

BEVERLY HEMBRECHT

ISBN 978-1-63525-294-1 (Paperback)
ISBN 978-1-63525-295-8 (Digital)

Copyright © 2016 by Beverly Hembrecht

All rights reserved. No part of this publication may be reproduced, distributed, or transmitted in any form or by any means, including photocopying, recording, or other electronic or mechanical methods without the prior written permission of the publisher. For permission requests, solicit the publisher via the address below.

Christian Faith Publishing, Inc.
296 Chestnut Street
Meadville, PA 16335
www.christianfaithpublishing.com

Printed in the United States of America

It was a bad time in my life. I was told I had cancer behind my left eye. It was inoperable. It lay too close to my brain. I would probably lose my eye or the sight in that eye. If the cancer grew, I could die. I had to undergo chemo and radiation to get rid of the cancer. There were several procedures done to relieve the pressure on my eye. I was tired, frustrated, I would lose my hair and be laid up for some time. Barbara Matthews, a Stephen's minister, came to visit me, and we got to talking and seemed to hit it off right away. We cried together and prayed together. During this time, she told me stories about Gabby. I was fascinated by the stories. This is about the adventures of Gabby and the developing friendship between the two women—one, the Stephen's minister; the other (me), undergoing chemo and radiation for cancer.

I needed Barbara's stories to help me forget what I was going through. And it worked. Barbara met Gabby quite by accident while she was grooming the cemetery her family gave to the community where she lived. Barbara was weeding graves when she felt something plucking at her bottom. She swatted it, thinking it was a fly or gnat. When she turned around, she saw a Canadian goose nipping at her. She shooed it away, but it came back. She spoke to the goose. "Well, what do you want with me?" she asked. The goose looked at her and gabbled, walking on, mulling about the grasses. She thought it was looking for food.

"I'll call you Gabby," Barbara said. "Come on then, let's get something to eat." She went to the maintenance building, took out some cracked corn, and fed the goose. It gobbled up the food and gabbled at Barbara. It was the beginning of a long, if somewhat adventurous, friendship.

As Barbara related the adventures of Gabby, our friendship grew deeper, more meaningful. When she came to see me, I was down. By the time she left, I was up-spirited and full of the desire to write the stories about the goose. We started to write about the goose. The goofy goose who didn't fit the bill as far as gooses go. Instead of flying with the flock, he followed Barbara around the cemetery. She talked to him, and he gabbled back at her day after day.

Barbara's husband was undergoing some health issues, and Barb was concerned for him. He also worked at the cemetery. He became familiar with the goose and his habit of following Barbara. Barbara didn't know where the goose was from or where it belonged. She just knew it kept coming to the cemetery, following her around. It seemed puzzling that the goose did not follow the flock when they flew off the lake. The goose often flew away and was gone for a day or two and Barbara thought it was gone for good when there it was

THE GIFT OF GABBY

again. One day while Barbara was working near the maintenance building, she heard a car down by the lake. Suddenly the goose flew toward the car, landing just short of the woman getting out of the car. The goose was squawking, gabbling a mile a minute. The woman laughed and called him Gabby. She appeared delighted to see the goose. Barbara watched from a distance, realizing this woman knew the goose. Barbara, being curious, walked down to the lady and introduced herself. The lady's name was Rachel. Rachel explained how she knew the goose. She told Barbara that she and her husband had raised Gabby and had wondered what had happened to him. He had flown away from their home and did not come back.

Now she understood where he had gone when he left. Barbara told her Gabby was following her around the cemetery every day. Rachel explained that she and her husband were out riding when her horse stepped into a nest of eggs. One egg was not broken, so they took it home and put it in a little box of cotton, under a lamp for heat, and waited for it to hatch. When it hatched, they kept the tiny goose alive with a vet's help. They raised the bird in their home. The little bird gabbled so much they named it Gabby. Rachel said that Gabby learned to fly in the house. It was a disaster area when he finally landed the first few times he flew. When Barbara told me the carnage involved with the bird's escapades in the house, I laughed till the tears ran. It was good therapy for me. We laughed and forgot the chemo and radiation therapy for those hours together. I will always treasure the time we spent as she reminisced about Gabby.

Not only did the stories take me away from memories of the first visit to the radiology department at the hospital with the pain involved in that first visit. I had to lie perfectly still for over an hour while my face was covered with a mesh screen fitted tightly to make a mask.

After it was dry, it was marked so the radiologist could send the laser into the area needing to be radiated. If they missed or I moved, I could be blinded or worse. This was painful since my left eye bulged out and I could not move. The mesh mask was fastened to a board under my head, which fastened me to it.

After all measurements and markings were done, the radiation was applied. After the first session, it was just a matter of coming in every day, being fitted with the mask, then radiated. It didn't take as long as the first day. On Fridays, after radiation, I went to the Cancer Center and had chemo for about two hours. This procedure was done with an IV. Afterward, I went home and climbed in bed and stayed for the night.

At the beginning, we had to go to Chapel Hill, where the doctor in charge was located. It was a four-hour drive, an all-day type of procedure. I went from one department to another for tests and procedures.

My doctor took a hose with a light on it up my nose to take pictures of my sinuses. I had PET Scans and CT Scans. He had other doctors-in-training in to take a look, since my case was so unusual. I hated this procedure since I had to be numb so I could do it. A gauze pad with something on it was placed up my nose to numb it; then he would take that light up there and take pictures.

Every time he asked me to sit in that chair, I said, "He's going up my nose with the rubber hose again."

When we got back home, I was so exhausted, I fell into bed. This went on for months. There was so much medicine to take. Bill made a schedule for me so that I could remember which pills to take and when to take them. My appetite took a nosedive, and I quit eating and drinking. My mouth began to shed, everything hurt to eat, especially hot foods. I was dehydrated. My chemo doctor took me off chemo because of it and told me he was just going to give me liquids for hydration. If I didn't drink or was not better by tomorrow, he would put me in the hospital. Needless to say, I started drinking lots of water and still do. This was a very low period. Barbara kept visiting. We prayed together and talked. Since I liked writing and she wanted to have Gabby's story written, I took it on. The time we spent on stories about Gabby helped me forget the weakness and pain of radiation and chemo. They were so hilarious, we were laughing, and I was getting well. We believed the laughter was helping me.

Rachel told Barbara that she and her husband had left Gabby in the box in the house when they went to work in the morning. The goose had been trying his wings and finally was successful. When they returned that evening, their house was in a topsy-turvy mess.

The lamps were on the floor, shades missing or askew. Anything loose was on the floor, broken. When the door opened, the goose flew outside, soared across the field, then turned back, and landed on the doorstep. He gabbled at them. So they decided to let Gabby out when they went to work each day. He could fly away if he wanted to. That was when he decided to adventure to the cemetery where Barbara worked.

Rachel told Barbara that, while they were raising Gabby, he followed them around and went where they went. He often jumped in the toilet to swim. He got in the shower with Rachel and flapped his wings, splattering water over the bathroom. Gabby was a member of the family. Since he liked the water, Cory filled an old wading pool with water for him. Gabby was flapping his wings, waiting for the pool to be filled. Cory called Rachel to come and see what fun Gabby was having.

She asked Gabby, "Want some company? Here I come!" When she jumped in the pool with him, she said, "Gabby, I bet you are the only Canadian goose in America with his own swimming pool!"

One weekend, they went to visit Cory's mom in High Point, North Carolina. They got in their car and started down the road. Suddenly, they heard a familiar squawking noise behind them.

When Cory looked in his rearview mirror, sure enough, Gabby was following. He wasn't flying. He was waddling as fast as his little feet would go, squawking, honking and gabbling, flapping his wings. Cory stopped the car. Gabby jumped in the backseat as if he belonged there. He jumped into the back window, looking out at the countryside. Rachel said people stared at the goose in their back window. A man stopped and scratched his head as if he didn't believe what he was seeing. Rachel said, "Won't Mom be surprised when she sees Gabby?"

When Cory and Rachel took Gabby to visit Cory's mom, she was surprised to see a goose waddling and honking through her front door. They asked if he could come inside. She said, "Okay, but I hope he doesn't make a mess." She filled a bowl with water and broke up some bread and put it on a plate and set everything on the floor for Gabby. She asked, "Will he be all right here in the house if we go to the store and do some shopping? It shouldn't take very long."

Cory answered, "Yes, we won't be gone that long."

When they returned, Gabby was sitting in Grandma's rocking chair, looking out the window. There was a trail of bird droppings from the kitchen to the living room.

"I've got it," Rachel said, "I'm used to cleaning up after him. I just don't know how to get him housebroken."

Gabby got the attention that day. He had his picture taken with the neighbor children. He waddled up and down the porch, puffing out his feathers like a mayor about to give a speech. Gabby settled into the back window on the way home that evening. He was so tired he almost fell off his seat in the window.

The next morning, they were late. They had forgotten to set the alarm. The rush was on to get showers and breakfast before leaving. Gabby waddled back and forth, squawking and gabbling, looking for food. Rachel grabbed a slice of bread and tore it up. She set it down for Gabby. He gobbled it up, squawking for more. Rachel tore up another slice of bread, muttering, "You are a spoiled little bird."

She shook her head and finished buttering her toast and grabbed a glass of juice. Rachel hurried to the shower with Gabby right behind her, jumping into the shower too. Rachel shouted, "Come and get him out of here. He's making a mess." Gabby was flapping his wings and dancing around while the water sprayed, and he flipped water over the bathroom. Cory came in and grabbed Gabby while munching on toast. He slid across the slippery floor with a towel, trying to mop as he slid along.

"This goose is going to drive me crazy," Rachel murmured as she dried off.

"That's why he didn't go with the other geese. He thought he was a person. He didn't know any better," Barbara explained as she told the story. I couldn't help but laugh every time another story unfolded. While we explored the possibilities for the stories about Gabby, my radiation and chemo continued. I remember the day I went to the beauty parlor and had to tell her to take my hair, or what was left of it, off. She was so kind and brought out some wigs for me to try. Somehow, I got through and went home. I must have cried for an hour. I didn't know how vain I was about my hair until that day. My poor husband just held me and let me cry. I hated wigs, but we tried to find one that I could tolerate. I wore scarves and caps around the house but needed at least one wig for when we went to the doctor, shopping, or church. I used the time in radiation to pray. I prayed for healing, for strength, and for everyone who was helping me to live. I learned to lean on Jesus and let go.

THE GIFT OF GABBY

I hated the long trips to Chapel Hill to see Dr. Weissler, who was in charge of my cancer treatment. It is a teaching hospital. Since my case was so rare, he called associates in to witness the procedures he was doing for me. The hospital was very large, and it was like a maze. We went from floor to floor and around the halls. It seemed endless.

We had appointments in several places. This meant getting there on the prescribed times. Sometimes, we had to wait, but most times, it was rushing from one department to another.

I was sick and tired all the time. Somehow we got to the places we needed to be because Bill (my husband) dragged me by the hand, hauling me from place to place. Then there was the long drive back home. It took us about four and a half hours. After sleeping for hours on end, I would start the whole procedure all over again. Then Barbara came, and we settled in the den to talk about Gabby. It was a great day when she regaled me with the antics of this goose. Each story was memorable and equally funny.

Here is another adventure in which Gabby was the central character. Gabby learned how to fly. After the disaster inside the house, Cory and Rachel let Gabby outside during the day while they were at work. On that first morning, they got in the car and started down the old dirt road. Gabby ran along behind and took flight. He soared over the car as it wound its way along toward the Old Liberty Road. They looked out the window and watched Gabby turn back toward home on his morning outing. The old car puttered along in the morning sunshine toward Greensboro, North Carolina. They passed the local post office where the postman was leaving for his daily run. They blew their horn and waved at the postman. He, knowing them, smiled and waved back.

THE GIFT OF GABBY

As they moved past the cemetery, they noticed the cars at the Julian Gas Station. The locals stopped here for gas and groceries, since the little grocery store was next door. A spunky, tiny redheaded female was the owner of the gas station. She was known to have a weapon nearby for safety. She knew how to use it, and almost everybody knew it. She was highly respected in the community. She was always fair with her customers as long as they were respectful. This was the place where the locals came to catch up on the latest gossip or news.

In the meantime, Gabby was flying farther and farther from home and returning in late afternoon. He flew from pond to pond, then settled on the pond in the cemetery. It was his routine, but he seemed to like the cemetery and the pond there more than anyplace.

One evening, after working late, the couple returned home, but Gabby was not there waiting. They wondered what happened to the goose. Several neighbors got in their cars and went looking for Gabby. Rachel worried and paced. Cory got on the phone and called several places to ask if they had seen Gabby. No one had seen the Canadian goose. Gabby had found a new friend in Barbara and her husband. He liked the pond in the cemetery and swam there on hot days. But he liked following Barbara around while she weeded or mowed. Barbara talked to Gabby about anything and everything. Gabby became a permanent part of her days.

The people knew Gabby as Barbara's pet goose. Barbara spoke about Gabby as if the goose were a person instead of a Canadian goose. I listened and took notes, and sometimes we just laughed about all the adventures Gabby brought into her life. She told me it was a time in her life when she needed something special. I never learned what was going on in her life then, but I assumed her husband was at the center of it. Since my own life was being put on hold, I often felt overwhelmed by my own circumstances. We never went there in conversations. We became friends. She was a special person in my life. I looked forward to her visits. I knew that she could always make my day. So Gabby became a good friend to me as well.

THE GIFT OF GABBY

Barbara told me about a day they had an unwelcome visitor. It was a beautiful, warm afternoon, and Barbara didn't feel like cutting grass. Lying down in the grass, she stretched out her arms and looked up at the blue Carolina sky. She lay there for quite a while and finally fell asleep. Suddenly, she felt something pecking at her pant leg. She opened her eyes to find Gabby sitting beside her like a watchdog.

"Okay, Okay, I will go back to work. But, Gabby, you must stay out of the way of the mower!" she exclaimed.

Gabby waddled down to the pond, nibbling the grass as he ambled along. When Barbara started the mower, Gabby started honking and flapping his wings. She hurriedly turned the mower off and ran toward Gabby, seeing that he was having trouble. She looked in the grass and saw something moving.

"Oh, oh! Sam! Sam!" Barbara shouted. She was barely able to take a breath. Sam came out of the barn at the sound of fear in Barbara's voice.

"Shovel! Shovel! Hurry, hurry," she said. A long water moccasin was trying to swallow the largest frog Barbara had ever seen. It was hanging out of the snake's mouth, his eyes bulging and croaking to get free. Sam came running with the shovel and raised it over the snake. "Oh, Sam, please be careful," Barbara said.

Sam replied, "Oh, God help me," and, with a deep breath, raised the shovel and heaved it at the snake's head. With a large *wham!* the snake was smashed, and the frog flew from the snake's mouth to freedom. "I've never seen such a happy frog." Barbara laughed. "Maybe now he will turn into a prince."

"I doubt that," Sam muttered.

The two were standing there with Gabby looking on.

Barbara said, "Thank you, Gabby, for the warning." Gabby just waddled into the pond and swam away.

My radiation treatments continued, along with chemo each Friday afternoon. One day, I was in the kitchen looking for a certain pan to do some baking. I went down to the floor to search in the bottom of a cupboard for the pan. When I tried to get up, I found that I was too weak to push myself up with my arms. I sat there for a while and tried again. No, I just could not get up. My phone was in the other room. I sat there for a little while, contemplating my situation. I could sit here for the rest of the day and wait for Bill to get home from work, or I could do something. I didn't realize that the treatments made me so weak and fragile. At first I started to panic, then decided that wasn't a good idea. I sat up straighter and scooted, on my bottom, toward the living area. I finally managed to get to the sofa and leaned my head on the seat of the sofa. I backed up and slowly scooted up to the seat backward. I was sitting on the sofa, hurrah for me! Now I could get up and go anywhere I wanted. It definitely scared me to think how weak I was due to the treatments for cancer. But thanks to God for answering all the prayers being said for me. I believed that I was getting better every day. I did not know what the residual effects of this would be. No one talked about side effects.

THE GIFT OF GABBY

Barbara and I kept up our conversations about Gabby and all his adventures. Barbara and her present husband, Larry, asked us out to dinner, and we gladly accepted the invitation. They also took us to the cemetery where her son worked, and we also visited the gas station and grocery.

We went to High Point, where Gabby was well-known. It helped to see the places she described when she talked about Gabby. The stories continued...

On this particular morning, nothing was going right for Sam and Barbara. They were trying to get to the cemetery early so that they could get the mowing done before it got too hot to be out in the sun. The morning started out very differently. The phone was ringing. Sam answered it with his usual, "Good morning."

"This is Kay, down at the filling station," the female voice said. "Please may I speak to Barbara?" she asked. Sam handed the phone to his wife, saying, "Kay's calling you."

"Good morning, Kay, what's happening?" Barbara asked, knowing Kay didn't call unless there was a problem at the cemetery. This time, however, the problem wasn't at the cemetery. "Can you come down here as soon as possible?" Kay asked.

"What is wrong, Kay?" Barbara asked.

"Well, Gabby is down here, and the delivery trucks are everywhere, and we are afraid he will get run over," Kay's frantic voice exclaimed.

"All right, I'm so sorry. I'll be there as soon as I can," Barbara replied. "Sam, I have to go. Gabby is in trouble at the gas station. Kay needs us to come and take him back to the cemetery. What are we going to do with that bird?"

"Well, we can't put him in a cage," Sam retorted. "He thinks he's a person and loves all the attention he gets. He's very different, you know."

"I know." Barbara agreed. "But I don't want anything to happen to him. He's my buddy, and I love him."

They got in the little red truck and headed for the gas station. By the time Barbara and Sam arrived, the problem had already been solved. The semidriver who delivered beer to the grocery was just getting into the big beer truck. Right beside him sat Gabby. Gabby stood like a king in the passenger seat looking out the window of the beer truck. Across the side of the window was a notice that read, "No passengers other than employees of the company."

Since Gabby was not an ordinary passenger, the driver did not think it wrong to take him back to his pond at the cemetery. Gabby strutted on the seat, honking and gabbling as the huge truck made its way down the street toward the pond near the cemetery. He was in his glory, riding in the beer truck with the driver grinning and shaking his head at the goose.

When the truck stopped, the driver got out and went around and opened the passenger door, saying, "Here you are, your majesty. Gabby, you are some kind of goose!" He scratched his head and climbed back in his truck. Gabby gabbled and honked a good-bye and waddled to the pond without looking back.

THE GIFT OF GABBY

Another story Barbara told me was so funny I just about choked on my cup of tea. I laughed so much. She said she finally had a day off and was preparing to do her housework when the phone rang. She thought, now what?

She picked up the phone and said, "Hello!"

The answer was, "Barbara, this is Jonny." Jonny was a neighbor who lived a short distance behind the filling station.

"Jonny, what do you want? Is something the matter?" Barbara asked.

"I have a small problem down here," Jonny said. "Your goose is down here at my house. What should I do with him?"

"Oh, just leave him alone. He will go back to the cemetery," Barbara replied.

"But, Barbara, he's in my house," Johnny said.

"Your house, how did he get in there?" Barbara asked. "I just opened the door, and he waddled right into the kitchen. I gave him some crackers, and then he waddled into my bathroom. I was running a bath in the tub with bubbles, and he jumped in. He's having a ball, taking my bath!" Jonny complained.

"Oh, Jonny, I'm so sorry. He won't hurt you. Can you handle him?" Barbara asked. "Yeah, I think I can take care of this. I just wanted to know what you wanted me to do. He's so cute in there. This is so funny. I don't believe this goose!" Jonny replied.

Gabby was thoroughly enjoying his bath and swam around amidst the bubbles, honking and gabbling as if he belonged there. But Jonny wanted to take her own bath. She sat on the side of the tub, getting sprinkled with Gabby's bathwater as he flapped his wings and splattered away!

Jonny allowed Gabby his bath, and after he had flapped his wings, slopping water all over the floor, Jonny shooed him outside and mopped up the mess in the bathroom.

When Sam came home that day, Barbara told him about Gabby's trip to Jonny Barnes's house. Sam said, "I wonder what other troubles he's gotten into that we don't know about. He often goes to the post office to see everyone who goes there."

Gabby's travels took him all over town from the feed mill to the gas station, grocery store, post office, and other people's ponds. But he always seemed to end up at the cemetery with Barbara. Many days when Barbara left in the little red truck, she would look behind and see Gabby running behind and then soaring over the cab. These stories brought a fresh breath to me and kept my thoughts busy while I got treated for my cancer. Even though I was sick and tired most days, when we got together, I looked forward to the many stories about Gabby. He became my hero. His antics took over while we chatted, and I forgot, for a time, what was happening to me. We worked on stories about Gabby. We laughed and I found that Barbara was a wonderful Christian who really cared about others more than herself. She gave fully of herself and shared so many "Gabby antics" it took away any sad thoughts of losing my eye or my life.

The next story about Gabby came as a surprise because we had been talking about losing things, which reminded Barbara of a day when Gabby wasn't there in the morning. Nothing wakes a person better than the aroma of fresh brewed coffee. It woke Barbara better than the alarm clock by her bed. Her feet hit the floor as she inhaled the wonderful aroma of fresh coffee.

"Come on, Sam, we have to get to the cemetery and get done before it gets too hot!" she exclaimed, pulling on jeans and a lightweight shirt.

They hurried to get the morning chores done and quickly loaded the little red truck with grass trimmers and water. The truck bed was filled with milk jugs filled with water for the flowers, since there were no water spigots in the cemetery. This was heavy work watering the planted beds of flowers by hand, but the blooms would be beautiful and worth the hard work. As they approached, the gas station Barbara noticed that Gabby was missing. He always seemed to come out of nowhere, flying an escort into the cemetery with them. Sam could never figure out where Gabby spent his nights. He left the cemetery when they left and returned the next morning. Gabby recognized the sound of the truck and waited for them. They thought Gabby had a special pond that he camped out on nearby. Gabby would recognize the sound of the truck and waited for them. But today, he wasn't waiting for them.

Sam looked around as he parked the truck in the shade of the pin oak tree. They shouted, almost together, "Gabby, Gabby!" But no answering gabble or honk returned.

Barbara croaked, "Something is wrong, Sam. I just feel it."

"Oh, maybe he just found a friend. Don't worry," he said. They got busy with their routine. Sam got on the mower after checking to be sure the gas tank was full.

Barbara was throwing cracked corn on the gravel for all the geese and ducks gathered there coming from places unknown. They were beautiful as they flew onto the pond, touching down while flapping their wings, then running up the bank to the barn where they knew their breakfast was waiting.

Barbara smiled. "You are so beautiful. Have a good breakfast." She put the bag of corn away and started her weed trimmer and began cutting the grass around the grave markers. As she was working her way around the first area, she looked up and saw Sam frantically waving his arms at her. She quickly turned off the trimmers and ran to him.

"What's wrong?" she shouted.

"I found Gabby," he replied. "Go slow. I think he's hurt."

Gabby was lying under a bush behind the barn. With tears flowing down Barbara's cheeks, she moaned, "Oh, no, Gabby, how did you get into this mess?" Barbara and Sam saw Gabby wrapped in fishing line and lying on his side, unable to move. They saw the fish hook snagged in his beak. Sam wrapped the goose in his arms while they worked together to free Gabby from the fishing line. He seemed to understand and lay still, allowing Sam and Barbara to free him. The hook was in the side of his beak. Sam carefully removed the ugly hook, and Gabby knew instantly that he was free. A tear slid silently down Sam's cheek as he pondered how this could have happened. "I bet I know what happened. Some fisherman left his cut fishing line lying on the ground down by the pond, and Gabby was down there and got all caught in it. The more he flapped around, the more tangled he got," Barbara said. "This makes me so angry. People can be so inconsiderate and careless about what they are doing to our wildlife." Gabby sat up, a bit wobbly on his legs, but hobbled away with a limp. They watched to make sure he was all right.

I could certainly relate to Gabby's experience. It reminded me of the first day of radiation when they had to make the mask and fit it to my face.

It seemed like it took hours for the whole procedure to be completed. First, they had to place the mask material over my face and, while it was wet, fit it tightly in order to make it like a cast, which is what it became. During this time, I had to lie completely still so that it would be exactly fitted to my face. I was trapped beneath that mask for hours. It had to dry, and then it had to be marked so the radiation went exactly to the tumor, behind my eye. If it was not done correctly, I could be damaged for life or killed by the radiation. It was a trap that had to be endured. So I could readily relate to Gabby's situation. And my heart went out to Gabby because he didn't know what had trapped him. But I had been told what was happening to me, even though I still hated the trapped feeling every time I had to be in the mask with my head fastened to a board. I had to lie still during radiation day after day, hoping for the best. I will never forget this experience or the wonderful, caring people who got me through it.

It was God Himself who got me through it because every day I had that time to pray. I learned to pray for so many others during that time. The Lord certainly hears our cries and sends the right people into our lives at the appropriate minute. Barbara had come into my life when I needed a friend to talk to. She brought Gabby into my life to light up my days and refresh my thoughts. I feel very blessed and thankful to God for giving me these friends and this time to pray.

The stories were real, and Barbara expressed the desire to have them written into a story. Gabby was a very close and dear friend whose antics clearly enthralled the listener. So we started writing stories about Gabby. I was smitten. I had already published a couple of books of poetry, with no noticeable results since I am terrible at marketing what I write. But this was a challenge I could not resist. Besides, while I was undergoing radiation and chemo for cancer, I thought it would be good to keep my mind busy and my fingers on the keyboard. At least I could do that without falling down or getting down and not being able to get up. The culminating story happened when Barbara and Sam were preparing for a funeral and burial at the cemetery. Gabby stayed close to Barbara all day as she set up for the funeral party at the grave site of Mr. Cole, who was a neighbor and friend.

"We have to make everything right for Mr. Cole, Gabby, just like we do for everyone who is buried here," Barbara said.

Gabby tilted his head as if he understood every word. It was lunchtime, and the sun was hot. Sam came from the grocery store and gas station, parking the truck in the shade of the pin oak tree. He brought oatmeal cookies and a pint of ice cream for each of them As they ate the ice cream with the little flat wooden spoons, Sam asked, "Why does this taste so much better down here than at home in a dish?"

"It's because you are hungry and it's like camping out in the woods," Barbara replied. "Gabby is acting strange. I wonder why."

The vault was placed over the grave. The American flag–draped casket was placed over the vault. The chairs were arranged in order. Sam, Barbara, and Gabby waited as the Cole family arrived to pay their final respects. Gabby waddled over to the front of the casket as the family went to their seats.

"Gabby, come here," Barbara whispered frantically. "Gabby, you are in the way." Gabby paid no attention to Barbara. He lifted his head up and started pecking at the flag, trying to pull it off the casket. Everyone noticed that Gabby was very nervous and upset. He waddled back and forth beside the casket, pecking at the American flag. As the minister prepared to say a prayer, Gabby walked over and stood beside the minister.

"Oh, Gabby, behave yourself." Barbara breathed.

Gabby paced around the grave during the entire service. The family appeared to understand what Gabby was doing. After the service, Barbara spoke to Mr. Cole's daughter, Morgan, apologizing for Gabby's strange intrusion.

"It was perfect that he stayed for my father's service," Morgan said. "My father would have loved knowing Gabby was here for him."

"He's never been that bold before. I am so embarrassed," Barbara replied.

"Don't be embarrassed. You don't understand. My father lived in a cabin on the lake. He fed the ducks and geese every day. He loved them," Morgan continued. "In his final days, he enjoyed walking down to the lake to watch the geese and ducks and wildlife. He told us about one special goose who stayed near him while he was fishing. At night, this goose would perch in an old tree near the water. He wondered why the goose was always by himself. He brought so much pleasure to my father's life. So you see, Gabby being at his funeral was just perfect."

Barbara reached over and gave Morgan a hug. "Thank you for explaining," she said.

Barbara turned and walked away, leaving Gabby by the graveside. Yes, there is something very special about this Canadian goose. Now she understood where Gabby had been when he wasn't with them at the cemetery, those missing days and nights.

It was very evident that Barbara cared a great deal for Gabby. I cared a great deal for both Barbara and Gabby. They saved my sanity and bolstered my faith like nothing else could. I will always cherish those memories.

This story doesn't end there. Was Gabby just a strange Canadian goose or someone or something sent from God to help some of us through some very tough spots in our lives? If he was just a goose, then why was he so funny and strange and uplifting? A coincidence? I don't think so.

Barbara's son, Mark, who takes care of the cemetery, is going through treatment a second time for cancer. I continued my radiation and chemo and graduated from those treatments. Dr. Weissler explained that surgery to find out if the cancer was really gone would be too radical for me to undergo but that the CT scans showed no signs of cancer. I have had several PET and CT scans since then, and no cancer has shown up. We moved to Illinois in 2010, where I have had another bout of cancer. This time it was uterine cancer, and I have a clean record as of my last visit to the surgeon. We are in prayer for Mark. Another thing, Mark received a letter from the White House, requesting some trees that are unique from the cemetery to be planted in Washington. So the trees, where Gabby wondered about, may go to Washington.

About the Author

Beverly has been writing for several years, but it is poetry, her first love. She's from Milford, Indiana, where she first started to write. She lives in Flora, Illinois, with her husband, Bill. They've been married for forty-two years and finish each other's sentences. She has two children, two grandchildren, and three great-grandchildren. Bev likes to quilt, crochet, garden, and write. She creates great apple dumplings and pies. This book is her first, and she is very pleased to have found a publisher who appreciates her work. This is a true story that Bev lived and survived cancer for a third time.